Zoo Keeper

Eleanor Archer

W
FRANKLIN WATTS
LONDON • SYDNEY

RNID
THE ROYAL NATIONAL
INSTITUTE FOR DEAF PEOPLE

Katy is a zoo keeper. She works with all the animals in the zoo.

Being deaf means sometimes having different ways of doing everyday things.

Katy is deaf. This means that she cannot hear very well. Katy wears a hearing aid to help her hear better. Some people who are deaf cannot hear anything at all.

Katy gets up at 6.30 a.m. and drives to the zoo. She starts work at 8 a.m. every day. There is a lot to do before the zoo opens.

When driving, both sight and sound are important. Deaf people who drive rely even more on their sight.

First Shaun, the head keeper, has a meeting with the other keepers. "Katy, can you clean out the parrots, please?" he asks.

Katy understands what Shaun is saying by lipreading. She watches the shape of Shaun's mouth as he speaks.

5

After the meeting, Katy collects a rake and bucket. She goes into the parrot enclosure to clean and rake the floor. She picks up any feathers the birds have dropped.

Next the keepers prepare breakfast for the lemurs. Lemurs eat vegetables and apples. "I'll clean out their sleeping area," Katy tells Sharon.

Then Katy puts some apple out for the lemurs. They are her favourite animals.

"Here you are!" she says. "Have some apple!"

On the way back from the
Lemur House, Katy sees Shaun.
They say hello to each other
by using a thumbs up sign.

Shaun uses
sign language.
This includes
handshapes,
movement
and expression.

Next Katy feeds the antelope.
Each animal in the zoo has
a carefully prepared diet.
When you visit a zoo it
is important not to
feed the animals.

**PLEASE
DO NOT FEED
OUR ANIMALS**

THEY RECEIVE A
BALANCED DIET
EXTRA FOOD
CAN BE HARMFUL

At 10.30 a.m. it's time for the keepers' tea break. "Do you think the parrot is settling in?" Katy asks Shaun. "It will take time," Shaun tells her.

After their break, Katy visits the new baby gibbon. It is important to check every day that the baby is healthy. Katy feeds the gibbons lettuce. This encourages them to come close to her so she can see them properly.

GIBBON

A baby was born on June 17th, 1999.

Shaun always knows where Katy is so that he can alert her if there is an emergency.

All through the day Shaun checks Katy's work. "Have you fed these tamarins?" he signs. "Yes," Katy answers with a nod.

The keepers have lunch at 12 o'clock and Katy eats with her friends. "Have you seen the baby gibbon yet?" Katy asks Geoff.

People who are deaf may not speak clearly because they do not hear how words should sound.

When you speak to a person who is lipreading it is important to look at them and speak clearly.

After lunch Katy helps with the tame animals in the Encounter Village. "What is the goat's name?" one boy asks. Katy shows him her badge which says that she is deaf and that she lipreads. "Her name's Splodge," she tells him.

Next Katy walks to the Giraffe House. "It's so hot, I must have an ice cream!" Katy thinks. She shows the attendant the one she wants. "Thanks!" Katy says as she pays for it.

Katy has a whistle she uses in emergencies. It attracts attention when people are far away from her.

When Katy arrives, it's treat time for the giraffes. They are hungry. "Steady on!" Katy thinks. "You'll knock me over!"

It's nearly the end of the day but there is still sweeping up to do. Katy and Sharon work together. Sharon taps Katy on the shoulder to get her attention. "We've finished!" she says.

To get a deaf person's attention, touch them gently so they know you are talking to them.

At 6 p.m. it's time for the keepers to go home.
Katy and Sharon are going to the cinema.
"Have a good time," Shaun tells them.
"See you tomorrow!"

So you want to be a zoo keeper?

1. You need to have a good basic education, followed by a City and Guilds course in Zoo Animal Management.

2. You need a real love and interest in animals and a sense of humour. Animals are hard work!

3. Remember you will work as part of a team as well as on your own.

4. Do you like lots of different animals, big and small, tame and scary? You will look after many different creatures.

5. There is a lot of cleaning up after the animals to do. Can you face it first thing in the morning?

6. Now you are ready to be a zoo keeper!

Facts about deafness

Your ear has three parts: the **outer ear** which is the part you can see, the **middle ear** and the **inner ear.** If any part is damaged, it can cause deafness.

There are different levels of deafness: **mild, moderate, severe** and **profound.**

A person who is **mildly deaf** finds it hard to hear a person speaking in a noisy place. They may wear a hearing aid that makes sounds louder.

A person who is **moderately deaf** may not hear unless they wear a hearing aid. They may lipread.

A person who is **severely deaf** may not hear much even if they wear a hearing aid. They probably lipread and may use sign language.

Someone who is **profoundly deaf** may lipread and may use sign language.

How you can help

When you speak to a person who lipreads, try to remember the following tips:

- Make sure the person is looking at you before you speak.

- Keep your hands away from your face and don't turn away while you are speaking.

- Be patient and take your time.

- Speak clearly and a little slower than usual.

- If the person asks you to repeat something, say it again using different words.

- Remember, deaf people are just like hearing people, except they can't hear!

Addresses and further information

The Royal National Institute for Deaf People (RNID)
19-23 Featherstone Street
London EC1Y 8SL
www.rnid.org.uk

National Deaf Children's Society
15 Dufferin Street
London EC1Y 8UR
www.ndcs.org.uk

National Centre for Learning and Literacy
The University of Reading
Bulmershe Court
Reading, RG6 1HY
www.ncll.reading.ac.uk

Australian Association of the Deaf
Suite 513, 149 Castlereagh Street
Sydney, NSW 2000
Australia
www.aad.org.au

Index

This edition 2004

Franklin Watts
96 Leonard Street
London
EC2A 4XD

Franklin Watts Australia
45-51 Huntley Street
Alexandria
NSW 2015

Copyright © 2000

ISBN: 0 7496 5587 9

Dewey Decimal Classification
Number: 362.4

10 9 8 7 6 5 4 3 2 1

A CIP catalogue record for
this book is available from the
British Library

Printed in Malaysia

Consultants: Anne Hodgson and Bridget
Middleton (RNID); Beverley Matthias (REACH)
Editor: Samantha Armstrong
Designer: Louise Snowdon
Photographer: Chris Fairclough
Illustrator: Derek Matthews

With thanks to: Katy Maroon, the keepers
and staff at Marwell Zoological Park,
Colden Common, Eastleigh; Gareth Moore,
St. Luke's Primary School, Westbeams Road, Sway,
Lymington, Hampshire.